Born in 1933

by

Kerry Butters.

Born in 1933

Millennium: **2nd millennium**

Centuries: 19th century – **20th century** – 21st century

Decades: 1900s 1910s 1920s – **1930s** – 1940s 1950s 1960s

Years: 1930 1931 1932 – **1933** – 1934 1935 1936

1933 (MCMXXXIII) was a common year starting on Sunday (dominical letter A) of the Gregorian calendar, the 1933rd year of the Common Era (CE) and *Anno Domini* (AD) designations, the 933rd year of the 2nd millennium, the 33rd year of the 20th century, and the 4th year of the 1930s decade.

Contents

Events

January

January 5: Golden Gate Bridge begun.

- January 5 – Construction of the Golden Gate Bridge begins in San Francisco Bay.
- January 11 – Sir Charles Kingsford Smith makes the first commercial flight between Australia and New Zealand.
- January 15 – Political violence causes almost 100 deaths in Spain.
- January 17 – The United States Congress votes favorably for Philippines independence, against the view of U.S. President Herbert Hoover.
- January 23 – The Twentieth Amendment to the United States Constitution is ratified, changing Inauguration Day from March 4 to January 20 starting in 1937.
- January 28 – *Pakistan Declaration*: Choudhry Rahmat Ali publishes (in Cambridge, England) a pamphlet entitled *Now or Never; Are We to Live or Perish Forever?* in which he calls for the creation of a Muslim state in northwest India that he calls "Pakstan" which is influential on the Pakistan Movement.
- January 30

- ○ Édouard Daladier forms a government in France.
- ○ Nazi leader Adolf Hitler is appointed Chancellor of Germany by President of Germany Paul von Hindenburg.
- ○ *The Lone Ranger* debuts on American radio.
- January – The London Underground diagram designed by Harry Beck is introduced to the public.

January 17: Vote on Philippines.

February

February 1 – Adolf Hitler gives his "Proclamation to the German People" in Berlin.

- February 2 – A second international conference on disarmament ends without results. It tries to limit the army sizes of the major powers, while Germany is entitled to 200,000; Germany leaves the conference because a plan postpones the limitations for 4 years.
- February 5 – A mutiny starts on the Royal Netherlands Navy coastal defence ship *De Zeven Provinciën* in the Dutch East Indies. After 6 days, it is bombed by a Dutch aircraft, killing 23, and the remaining mutineers surrender.
- February 6 – The Twentieth Amendment to the United States Constitution goes into effect.
- February 6–7 – Officers on the USS *Ramapo* record a 34-meter high sea-wave in the Pacific Ocean.
- February 9 – The King and Country debate: The Oxford Union student debating society in England passes a resolution stating, "That this House will in no circumstances fight for its King and country."
- February 10 – The New York City-based Postal Telegraph Company introduces the first singing telegram.
- February 15 – In Miami, Giuseppe Zangara attempts to assassinate President-elect Franklin D. Roosevelt, but instead fatally wounds the Mayor of Chicago, Anton Cermak.
-

- February 17
  - *Newsweek* magazine is published for the first time in the United States.
  - The Blaine Act passes the United States Senate, submitting the proposed Twenty-first Amendment to the Constitution to the states for ratification. The amendment is ratified on December 5, ending prohibition in the United States.
- February 27 – Reichstag fire: Germany's parliament building in Berlin, the Reichstag building, is set on fire under controversial circumstances.
- February 28 – The Reichstag Fire Decree is passed in response to the Reichstag fire, nullifying many German civil liberties.

March

- March 2 – The original film version of *King Kong*, starring Fay Wray, premieres at Radio City Music Hall and the RKO Roxy Theatre in New York City.
- March 3
  - Ching Yun University is established.
  - Mount Rushmore National Memorial is dedicated.
  - A powerful earthquake and tsunami hit Honshū, Japan, killing approximately 3,000 people.
- March 4
  - U.S. President Herbert Hoover is succeeded by Franklin D. Roosevelt (FDR), who in reference to the Great Depression, proclaims "The only thing we have to fear, is fear itself" in his inauguration speech. FDR is sworn in by Chief Justice Charles Evans Hughes. It is also the last time Inauguration Day in the United States occurs on March 4.
  - Frances Perkins becomes United States Secretary of Labor, and the first female member of the United States Cabinet.
  - The Parliament of Austria is suspended because of a quibble over procedure; Chancellor Engelbert Dollfuss initiates authoritarian rule by decree (see Austrofascism).
  -

- March 5
  - The Great Depression: President Franklin D. Roosevelt declares a "Bank holiday", closing all United States banks and freezing all financial transactions (the 'holiday' ends on March 13).
  - German election, 1933: National Socialists gain 43.9% of the votes.
- March 6 – Mayor Anton Cermak of Chicago dies of the wound he received on February 15.
- March 9 – Great Depression: The United States Congress begins its first 100 days of enacting New Deal legislation.
- March 10 – The 6.4 Mw Long Beach earthquake shakes Southern California with a maximum Mercalli intensity of VIII (*Severe*), killing 115 people.
- March 12 – Great Depression: Franklin Delano Roosevelt addresses the nation for the first time as President of the United States, in the first of his "Fireside chats".
- March 15
  - The Dow Jones Industrial Average rises from 53.84 to 62.10. The day's gain of 15.34%, achieved during the depths of the Great Depression, remains to date as the largest 1-day percentage gain for the index.
  - Austrian Chancellor Engelbert Dollfuss keeps members of the National Council from convening, starting the Austrofascist dictatorship.
- March 20 – Dachau, the first Nazi concentration camp, is completed (it opens March 22).
- March 22 – President Franklin Roosevelt signs an amendment to the Volstead Act known as the Cullen–Harrison Act, allowing the manufacture and sale of "3.2 beer" (3.2% alcohol by weight, approximately 4% alcohol by volume) and light wines.
- March 23 – The *Reichstag* passes the Enabling Act, making Adolf Hitler dictator of Germany.
- March 24 – Jewish protesters in New York City call for a boycott of German goods in response to the persecution of German Jews by the Nazis.

- March 27 – Japan announces to leave the League of Nations (due to a cancelation period of exactly two years, the egression becomes effective March 27, 1935)
- March 31 – The Civilian Conservation Corps is established with the mission of relieving rampant unemployment in the United States.

April

- April 1 – The recently elected Nazis under Julius Streicher organize a one-day boycott of all Jewish-owned businesses in Germany.
- April 2 – In a cricket test match against New Zealand, England batsman Wally Hammond scores a record 336 runs.
- April 3
    - An anti-monarchist rebellion occurs in Siam (Thailand).
    - First flight over Mount Everest, a British expedition, led by the Marquis of Clydesdale, and funded by Lucy, Lady Houston.

February 27: Reichstag fire.

- April 4 – The American airship *Akron* crashes off the coast of New Jersey, killing 73 of its 76 crewmen. It is the worst aviation accident in history up to this date and until 1950.

- April 5
  - The International Court of Justice in The Hague decides that Greenland belongs to Denmark and condemns Norwegian landings on eastern Greenland. Norway submits to the decision.
  - President of the United States Franklin D. Roosevelt declares a national emergency and issues Executive Order 6102, making it illegal for U.S. citizens to own substantial amounts of monetary gold or bullion.
- April 7
  - Sale of some beer is legalized in the United States under the Cullen-Harrison Act of March 22, eight months before the full repeal of Prohibition in December.
  - The Law for the Restoration of the Professional Civil Service is passed in Germany, the first law of the new regime directed against Jews (as well as political opponents).
- April 11 – Aviator Bill Lancaster takes off in England, in an attempt to make a speed record to the Cape of Good Hope, but vanishes (his body is not found in the Sahara Desert until 1962).
- April 13 – The Children and Young Persons Act is passed in the United Kingdom.
- April 19 – The United States officially goes off the gold standard.
- April 21 – Nazi Germany outlaws the kosher ritual shechita.
- April 24
  - Persecution of Jehovah's Witnesses in Nazi Germany begins with seizure of the Bible Students' office in Magdeburg.
  - Jewish physicians in Nazi Germany are excluded from official insurance schemes, forcing many to give up their practices.
- April 26
  - The Gestapo secret police are established in Nazi Germany by Hermann Göring.
  - Editors of the *Harvard Lampoon* steal the Sacred Cod of Massachusetts from the State House (it is returned two days later).

- April 27
    - The Jessop & Son department store in Nottingham, England is acquired by John Lewis Partnership (its first store outside of London).
    - The Stahlhelm organization joins the Nazi party.

May

- May 2
    - The first alleged modern sighting of the Loch Ness Monster occurs.
    - *Gleichschaltung*: Adolf Hitler prohibits trade unions.

- May 3
    - In the Irish Free State, Dáil Éireann abolishes the oath of allegiance to the British Crown.
    - Nellie Tayloe Ross becomes the first woman to be named director of the United States Mint.
- May 5 – The detection by Karl Jansky of radio waves from the center of the Milky Way Galaxy is reported in the *New York Times*. The discovery leads to the birth of radio astronomy.
- May 8 – Mohandas Gandhi begins a 3-week hunger strike because of the mistreatment of the lower castes.
- May 10
    - In Germany, the Nazis stage massive public book burnings.
    - Paraguay declares war on Bolivia.
- May 12 – Agricultural Adjustment Act is enacted in the USA.
- May 17 – Vidkun Quisling and Johan Bernhard Hjort form The Nasjonal Samling (the National-Socialist Party) of Norway.
- May 18 – New Deal: President Franklin Delano Roosevelt signs an act creating the Tennessee Valley Authority.
- May 26 – The Nazi Party in Germany introduces a law to legalize eugenic sterilization.

- May 27
    - New Deal: The Federal Securities Act is signed into law, requiring the registration of securities with the Federal Trade Commission.
    - The *Century of Progress* World's Fair opens in Chicago.
    - Walt Disney's classic *Silly Symphony* cartoon *The Three Little Pigs* is first released by United Artists.

June

- June 5 – The U.S. Congress abrogates the United States' use of the gold standard by enacting a joint resolution nullifying the right of creditors to demand payment in gold.
- June 6 – The first drive-in movie theater opens in Pennsauken Township, near Camden, New Jersey.
- June 12 – The London Economic Conference is held.
- June 17 – Union Station massacre: In Kansas City, Missouri, Pretty Boy Floyd kills an FBI agent, 3 local police, and the person they intended to rescue, captured bank robber Frank Nash.
- June 21 – All non-Nazi parties are forbidden in Germany.
- June 25 – Wilmersdorfer Tennishallen delegates convene in Berlin to protest against the persecution of Jehovah's Witnesses in Nazi Germany.
- June 26 – The *American Totalisator Company* unveils its first electronic pari-mutuel betting machine at the Arlington Park race track near Chicago.

July

- July 1 – The London Passenger Transport Board is founded.
- July 4 – Gandhi is sentenced to prison in India.
- July 6 – The first Major League Baseball All-Star Game is played at Comiskey Park in Chicago.

- July 8 – The first rugby union test match is played between the Wallabies of Australia and the Springboks of South Africa at Newlands in Cape Town.
- July 14 – In Nazi Germany:
  - Formation of new political parties is forbidden.
  - The Law for the Prevention of Hereditarily Diseased Offspring is enacted, allowing compulsory sterilization of citizens suffering from a list of alleged genetic disorders.
- July 15
  - Signing of the Four-Power Pact by Britain, France, Germany and Italy.
  - International Left Opposition (ILO) is renamed International Communist League (ICL).
- July 20 – Reichskonkordat: Vatican state secretary Eugenio Pacelli (later Pope Pius XII) signs an accord with Germany.
- July 22
  - Wiley Post becomes the first person to fly solo around the world, landing at Floyd Bennett Field in Brooklyn, New York, after traveling eastabout 15,596 mi (25,099 km) in 7 days 18 hours 45 minutes.
  - "Machine Gun Kelly" and Albert Bates kidnap Charles Urschel, an Oklahoma oilman, and demand $200,000 ransom.
- July 24 – Several members of the Barrow Gang are injured or captured during a running battle with local police near Dexter, Iowa.

August

- August 1 – The Blue Eagle emblem of the National Recovery Administration is displayed publicly for the first time.
- August 2 – Opening of the Stalin White Sea–Baltic Sea Canal, a 227 km navigable waterway constructed using forced labour in the Soviet Union connecting the White Sea with Lake Onega and the Baltic.

- August 7 – Simele massacre: More than 3,000 Assyrian Iraqis are killed by Iraq government troops.
- August 12 – Winston Churchill makes his first public speech warning of the dangers of German rearmament.
- August 14 – Loggers cause a forest fire in the Coast Range of Oregon, later known as the first forest fire of the Tillamook Burn. It is extinguished on September 5, after destroying 240,000 acres (970 km^2).
- August 25 – The Diexi earthquake shakes Mao County, Sichuan, China and kills 9,000 people.
- August 30 – German Jewish philosopher Theodor Lessing is assassinated in Marienbad (Mariánské Lázně), Czechoslovakia, dying the following day.

September

- September 3 – Alejandro Lerroux forms a new government in Spain.
- September 12 – Leó Szilárd, waiting for a red light on Southampton Row in Bloomsbury, conceives the idea of the nuclear chain reaction.
- September 26 – A hurricane destroys the town of Tampico, Mexico.

October

- October 1 – A failed assassination attempt against Engelbert Dollfuss, leader of the Fatherland's Front in Austria, seriously injures him.
- October 7 – Air France is formed by the merger of five French airline companies, beginning operations with 250 planes.
- October 10 – 1933 United Airlines Boeing 247 mid-air explosion: A bomb destroys a United Airlines Boeing 247 on a transcontinental flight in mid-air near Chesterton, Indiana, killing

all 7 on board, in the first proven case of sabotage in civil aviation, although no suspect is ever identified.

- October 12 – The United States Army Disciplinary Barracks on Alcatraz is acquired by the United States Department of Justice, which plans to incorporate the island into its Federal Bureau of Prisons as a federal penitentiary.
- October 13 – The British Interplanetary Society is founded.
- October 14 – Germany announces its withdrawal from the League of Nations and the World Disarmament Conference, after the U.S., the U.K. and France deny its request to increase its defense armaments under the Versailles Treaty.
- October 14-16 – A new Constitution of Estonia is approved only on the third consecutive referendum.
- October 17 – Scientist Albert Einstein arrives in the United States where he settles permanently as a refugee from Nazi Germany and takes up a position at the Institute for Advanced Study, Princeton, New Jersey.

November

- November 5 – Spanish Basque people vote for autonomy.
- November 8 – New Deal: U.S. President Franklin D. Roosevelt unveils the Civil Works Administration, an organization designed to create jobs for more than 4 million of the unemployed.
- November 11 – Dust Bowl: In South Dakota, a very strong dust storm, ("the great black blizzard"), strips topsoil from desiccated farmlands (one of a series of disastrous dust storms that year).
- November 16 – The United States and the Soviet Union establish formal diplomatic relations.
- November 17 – The Marx Brothers' anarchic comedy film *Duck Soup* is released in the U.S.
- November 19 – Second Spanish Republic: General elections result in victory by the right-wing parties.
- November 22 – The Fujian People's Government is declared in Fujian Province, China.

December

- December 5 – The 21st Amendment to the United States Constitution is passed, repealing Prohibition.
- December 15 – The US 21st Amendment officially goes into effect, alcohol becomes legal in the US.
- December 21
  - Newfoundland returns to Crown colony status following financial collapse.
  - The British Plastics Federation (the oldest in the world) is founded.
- December 24 – A train crash in Lagny, France kills over 200.
- December 26
  - The Nissan Motor Company is organized in Tokyo, Japan.
  - FM radio is patented.
- December 29 – Members of the Iron Guard assassinate Ion Gheorghe Duca, prime minister of Romania.

Date unknown

- The United States Federal Government outlaws cannabis.
- A coup attempt against Franklin Delano Roosevelt fails in the United States (*see* Smedley Butler).
- US President Roosevelt rejects socialism and government ownership of industry.
- Nazi Germany forms the *Expert Committee on Questions of Population and Racial Policy* under Reich Interior Minister Wilhelm Frick.
- The Holodomor genocide takes place in Ukraine.
- The first doughnut store under the Krispy Kreme name opens in Nashville, Tennessee.
- Jimmie Angel becomes the first foreigner to see the Angel Falls, Venezuela (they are named after him).
- The *Adélaïde Concerto*, a spurious work attributed to Wolfgang Amadeus Mozart, is published as "edited" (actually composed) by Marius Casadesus.

- 15 million unemployed in the USA.
- Five coalition cabinets form and fall in France.
- Turkey concludes a treaty with the creditors of the former Ottoman Empire to schedule the payments in Paris. (Turkey succeeds in clearing all the debt in less than twenty years.)
- The first dated ISCF group is started in Australia at North Sydney Boys High School, with the group still running today.
- English cricket team in Australia in 1932–33: The England cricket team wins The Ashes using the controversial bodyline tactic.
- The Mexican Indian Wars end after 414 years.

Births

January

- January 2
  - On Kawara, Japanese conceptual artist (d. 2014)
  - Morimura Seiichi, Japanese novelist and author
- January 6
  - Oleg Makarov, Russian cosmonaut (d. 2003)
  - Emil Steinberger, Swiss comedian, director, and writer
- January 8 – Charles Osgood, American journalist and commentator
  - Jean-Marie Straub, French filmmaker
- January 9 – Robert García, American politician
- January 14 – Stan Brakhage, American filmmaker (d. 2003)
- January 16 – Susan Sontag, American author (d. 2004)
- January 17
  - Dalida, French singer (d. 1987)
  - Prince Sadruddin Aga Khan, French U.N. High Commissioner for Refugees (d. 2003)
- January 18 – John Boorman, English film director
- January 23 – Chita Rivera, American actress and dancer
- January 25 – Corazon Aquino, President of the Philippines (d. 2009)

February

Kim Novak

Nina Simone

- February 2
  - M'el Dowd, American actress and singer (d. 2012)
  - Tony Jay, British-American actor (d. 2006)
- February 3 – Polde Bibič, Slovenian film and stage actor and memoir writer (d. 2012)
- February 6 – Leslie Crowther, British TV comedian & game show host (d. 1996)
- February 7 – John Anderton, English footballer
- February 8 – Elly Ameling, Dutch soprano
- February 12 – Costa-Gavras, Greek-born director and writer
- February 13
  - Paul Biya, President of Cameroon
  - Kim Novak, American film actress
- February 14 – Madhubala, Indian actress (d. 1969)
- February 17 – Craig L. Thomas, American Senator (d. 2007)
- February 18
  - Yoko Ono, Japanese-born singer and artist, widow of John Lennon
  - Sir Bobby Robson, English soccer player and manager (d. 2009)

- February 21 – Nina Simone, American singer (d. 2003)
- February 22 – Katharine, Duchess of Kent
- February 23 – Donna J. Stone, American poet and philanthropist (d. 1994)
- February 27 – Raymond Berry, American football player
- February 28 – Miro Steržaj, Slovenian bowler and businessman

March

Barbara Feldon

Abolhassan Banisadr

- March 3 – Lee Radziwill, American socialite, sister of Jacqueline Kennedy Onassis
- March 6 – Ted Abernathy, American baseball player (d. 2004)
- March 7 – Jackie Blanchflower, Northern Irish footballer (d. 1998)
- March 10 – Elizabeth Azcona Cranwell, Argentine poet and translator (d. 2004)
- March 12
  - Myrna Fahey, American actress (d. 1973)
  - Barbara Feldon, American actress and model

- ○ Jesús Gil, Spanish right-wing politician, construction businessman, and football team owner (d. 2004)
- March 13 – Mike Stoller, American songwriter
- March 14
  - ○ Sir Michael Caine, English actor
  - ○ René Felber, Swiss Federal Councilor
  - ○ Quincy Jones, American music producer and composer
- March 15 – Ruth Bader Ginsburg, U.S. Supreme Court Justice
- March 16 – Sandy Weill, American financier and philanthropist
- March 19 – Philip Roth, American author
- March 22 – Abolhassan Banisadr, first President of Iran
- March 27 _ Lê Văn Hưng South Vietnam army generals (d.1975)

April

Jean-Paul Belmondo

Elizabeth Montgomery

Willie Nelson

- April 1 – Claude Cohen-Tannoudji, French physicist and Nobel Prize laureate
- April 3 – Renae Youngberg. American professional baseball player
- April 5
  - Larry Felser, American sports columnist (d. 2014)
  - Frank Gorshin, American actor (*Batman*) (d. 2005)
- April 6 – Roy Goode, British legal academic
- April 7 – Wayne Rogers, American actor (d. 2015)
- April 9
  - Jean-Paul Belmondo, French actor
  - Gian Maria Volontè, Italian actor (d. 1994)
- April 12
  - Dame Montserrat Caballé, Catalan soprano
  - Ben Nighthorse Campbell, U.S. Senator
- April 14 – Morton Subotnick, American electronic composer
- April 15
  - Roy Clark, American country musician
  - Elizabeth Montgomery, American actress (*Bewitched*) (d. 1995)
- April 16 – Dame Joan Bakewell, British broadcaster
- April 18 – Michael Bradshaw, British actor (d. 2001)
- April 19 – Jayne Mansfield, American actress (d. 1967)
- April 24
  - Patricia Bosworth, American writer and biographer
  - Claire Davenport, British actress (d. 2002)
- April 25
  - Jerry Leiber, American composer (d. 2011)

- Joyce Ricketts, American baseball player [AAGPBL] (d. 1992)
- April 26
  - Carol Burnett, American actress, singer and comedian
  - Ilkka Kuusisto, Finnish composer
  - Arno Allan Penzias, German-born physicist, Nobel Prize laureate
- April 29
  - Mark Eyskens, Prime Minister of Belgium
  - Rod McKuen, American singer-songwriter and poet (d. 2015)
- April 30
  - Vittorio Merloni, Italian entrepreneur (d. 2016)
  - Willie Nelson, American country singer and songwriter

May

Joan Collins

- May 3
  - James Brown, African-American soul musician (*I Feel Good*) (d. 2006)
  - Steven Weinberg, American physicist, Nobel Prize laureate
- May 4 – J. Fred Duckett, Texan Sports announcer and teacher (d. 2007)
- May 7
  - Johnny Unitas, American football player (d. 2002)
  - Nexhmije Pagarusha, Albanian singer and actress
  - Roger Perry, American actor
- May 9 – Jessica Steele, English romance novelist
- May 10 – Barbara Taylor Bradford, English writer
- May 11 – Louis Farrakhan, African-American Muslim leader
- May 14 – Siân Phillips, Welsh actress

- May 15 – Carol Habben, American baseball player (d. 1997)
- May 21 – Maurice André, French trumpeter (d. 2012)
- May 22 – Chen Jingrun, Chinese mathematician (d. 1996)
- May 23
  - Joan Collins, English actress (*Dynasty*)
  - Shōzō Iizuka, Japanese voice actor
- May 25 – Ray Spencer, English footballer
- May 26 – Edward Whittemore, American writer and CIA agent (d. 1995)
- May 29 – Helmuth Rilling, German conductor

June

Joan Rivers

- June 1 – Charles Wilson, American politician (d. 2010)
- June 6 – Heinrich Rohrer, Swiss physicist, Nobel Prize laureate (d. 2013)
- June 8 – Joan Rivers, American comedic actress, comedian (d. 2014)
- June 11 – Gene Wilder, American actor
- June 14 – Vladislav Rastorotsky, Soviet gymnastics coach
- June 17
  - Harry Browne, American writer and Presidential candidate (d. 2006)
  - Maurice Stokes, American basketball player (d. 1970)
- June 19 – Viktor Patsayev, Russian cosmonaut (d. 1971)
- June 20 – Danny Aiello, American actor
- June 21 – Bernie Kopell, American actor and comedian
- June 23 – Dave Bristol, American baseball manager

- June 25 – Álvaro Siza, Portuguese Architect
- June 26 – Claudio Abbado, Italian conductor (d. 2014)
- June 29 – John Bradshaw, American theologian and educator

July

M. T. Vasudevan Nair

- July 2 – Kenny Wharram, Canadian ice hockey player
- July 6 – Frank Austin, English footballer (d. 2004)
- July 7
    - Murray Halberg, New Zealand runner
    - David McCullough, American historian and author
    - Bruce Wells, English boxer and actor (d. 2009)
- July 9 – Oliver Sacks, English-born neurologist (d. 2015)
- July 11 – Bob McGrath, American actor
- July 15
    - Guido Crepax, Italian comics artist (d. 2003)
    - Julian Bream, English guitarist and lutenist
    - M. T. Vasudevan Nair, Indian writer
- July 17 – Karmenu Mifsud Bonnici, 9th Prime Minister of Malta
- July 18
    - Syd Mead, American industrial and conceptual designer
    - Jean Yanne, French film actor and director (d. 2003)
- July 20
    - Buddy Knox, American singer (d. 1999)
    - Cormac McCarthy, Pulitzer Prize winning and National Book Award winning author
- July 21 – John Gardner, American novelist (d. 1982)
- July 23 – Bert Convy, American game show host, actor and singer (d. 1991)

- July 24
  - John Aniston, American actor
  - Doug Sanders, American former golfer
- July 26 – Kathryn Hays, American television and soap opera actress
- July 27
  - Nick Reynolds, American folk singer (d. 2008)
  - Ted Whitten, Australian rules footballer (d. 1995)
- July 28 – Charlie Hodge, Canadian former ice hockey goaltender
- July 29
  - Peter Baldwin, British actor
  - Lou Albano, American professional wrestler and actor (d. 2009)
  - Robert Fuller, American former actor and current rancher
- July 30 – Edd Byrnes, American actor and singer

August

- August 1
  - Dom DeLuise, American actor and comedian (d. 2009)
  - Jesse Corti, Venezuelan-born actor and comedian
- August 2 – Tom Bell, English actor (d. 2006)
- August 8 – Joe Tex, African-American soul singer (d. 1982)
- August 10 – Doyle Brunson, American poker player
- August 11 – Jerry Falwell, American evangelist and conservative political activist (d. 2007)
- August 14 – Richard R. Ernst, Swiss chemist, Nobel Prize laureate
- August 16
  - Julie Newmar, American actress
  - Stuart Roosa, American astronaut (d. 1994)
- August 17 – Gene Kranz, retired American NASA Flight Director
- August 18 – Roman Polanski, Polish film director
- August 19 – Bettina Cirone, American photographer and model
- August 20 – George J. Mitchell, former United States Senator
- August 21
  - Dame Janet Baker, English mezzo-soprano
  - Barry Norman, English film critic

- August 23 – Robert Curl, American chemist, Nobel Prize laureate
- August 25 – Tom Skerritt, American actor
- August 26 – Robert Chartoff, American film producer
- August 28 – Jean Weaver, American female professional baseball player (d. 2008)
- August 29 – Arnold Koller, Swiss Federal Councilor

September

Karl Lagerfeld

- September 1
  - Ann Richards, Governor of Texas (d. 2006)
  - T. Thirunavukarasu, Sri Lankan Tamil politician (d. 1982)
  - Conway Twitty, American country music artist (d. 1993)
- September 2 – Victor Spinetti, Welsh actor (d. 2012)
  - Mathieu Kérékou, President of Benin (d. 2015)
- September 9 – Michael Novak, American philosopher and author
- September 10 –
  - Yevgeny Khrunov, Russian cosmonaut (d. 2000)
  - Karl Lagerfeld, German fashion designer and artist
- September 11 – William Luther Pierce, American author and activist (d. 2002)
- September 13 – Eileen Fulton, American stage and soap opera actress
- September 14 – Hillevi Rombin, Miss Universe 1955 (d. 1996)
- September 15
  - Henry Darrow, Puerto-Rican American actor
  - Rafael Frühbeck de Burgos, Spanish conductor (d. 2014)
  - Monica Maughan, Australian actress (d. 2010)

- September 17 – Dorothy Loudon, American actress and singer (d. 2003)
- September 18
  - Scotty Bowman, Canadian ice hockey coach
- September 19 – David McCallum, Scottish actor
- September 20 – Dennis Viollet, English former footballer (d. 1999)
- September 21 – Dick Simon, American racing driver
- September 24
  - Raffaele Farina, Archivist of the Holy Roman Church and cardinal
  - Mel Taylor, American drummer (The Ventures) (d. 1996)
- September 25 – Hubie Brown, American basketball coach and broadcaster
- September 27
  - Greg Morris, American actor (d. 1996)
  - Kathleen Nolan, American actress and first female president of the Screen Actors Guild
  - Will Sampson, American actor (d. 1987)
- September 29 – Samora Machel, President of Mozambique (d. 1986)
- September 30 – Cissy Houston, American singer

October

- October 2 – John Gurdon, British developmental biologist, recipient of the Nobel Prize in Physiology or Medicine
- October 4 – German Moreno, Filipino television actor and host (d. 2016)
- October 9
  - Joan Berger, American female professional baseball player
  - Peter Mansfield, British physicist, recipient of the Nobel Prize in Physiology or Medicine
- October 10 – Jay Sebring, American hair stylist (d. 1969)
- October 10 – John Williams, Perth wrestler* October 17 – Jeanine Deckers, Belgian nun, known as "The Singing Nun" (d. 1985)
- October 12 – Clayton Jacobson II, American inventor of the Jet Ski.

- October 23 – Lois Youngen, American professional baseball player
- October 24
    - Reginald Kray, British gangster (d. 2000)
    - Ronald Kray, British gangster (d. 1995)
    - Norman Rush, American writer

November

Larry King

- November 1
    - Samir Roychoudhury, Indian Bengali poet and philosopher of Hungry generation
    - Huub Oosterhuis, Dutch poet, theologian and liturgy reformer
- November 3
    - John Barry, British film score composer (d. 2011)
    - Ken Berry, American actor
    - Jeremy Brett, British actor (d. 1995)
    - Aneta Corsaut, American actress (d. 1995)
    - Michael Dukakis, American politician and 1988 Democratic Presidential candidate
    - Amartya Sen, Indian economist, Nobel Prize laureate
- November 4 – Didier Ratsiraka, former President of Madagascar
- November 6 – Knut Johannesen, Norwegian speed-skater
- November 9 – Jim Perry, American game show host (d. 2015)
- November 10 – Don Clarke, Rugby football player of New Zealand (d. 2002)
- November 11 – Kay Arthur, American Bible teacher, speaker and author
- November 12 – Jalal Talabani, President of Iraq

- November 14 – Fred Haise, American astronaut who flew in Apollo 13
- November 15 – Jack Burns, American actor
- November 19 – Larry King, American talk show host
- November 21 – T. Rasalingam, Sri Lankan Tamil politician
- November 23 – Krzysztof Penderecki, Polish composer
- November 25 – Kathryn Grant, American actress
- November 26
  - Robert Goulet, American entertainer (d. 2007)
  - Tony Verna, American inventor of instant replay (d. 2015)
- November 28 – Hope Lange, American actress (d. 2003)
- November 29 – John Mayall, English singer

December

Akihito of Japan

- December 1
  - Fujiko F. Fujio, Japanese cartoon artist (d. 1996)
  - Lou Rawls, African-American singer (d. 2006)
- December 2 – Mike Larrabee, American athlete (d. 2003)
- December 3 – Paul J. Crutzen, Dutch chemist, Nobel Prize laureate
- December 4 – Wink Martindale, American game show host and disc jockey
- December 6 – Henryk Górecki, Polish composer (d. 2010)
- December 9 – Orville Moody, American golfer (d. 2008)
- December 11 – Charlie Bryan, American labor leader (d. 2013)
- December 15 – Tim Conway, American actor and comedian
- December 17

- o Shirley Abrahamson, American jurist; Chief Justice of the Wisconsin Supreme Court
  - o Walter Booker, American jazz bassist (d. 2006)
- December 20 – Jean Carnahan, American politician
- December 22 – Abel Pacheco, President of Costa Rica
- December 23 – Emperor Akihito of Japan
- December 26
  - o Ugly Dave Gray, Australian television personality
  - o Caroll Spinney, American puppeteer

Date unknown

- Augusto Odone, creator of *Lorenzo's Oil* (d. 2013)

Deaths

January–March

Wilhelm Cuno

Calvin Coolidge

- January 3
    - Wilhelm Cuno, Chancellor of Germany (b. 1876)
    - Jack Pickford, Canadian-born actor (b. 1896)
- January 5 – Calvin Coolidge, 30th President of the United States (b. 1872)
- January 7 – Bert Hinkler, Australian pioneer aviator (b. 1892)
- January 10 – Roberto Mantovani, Italian geologist (b. 1854)
- January 17 – Louis Comfort Tiffany, stained glass artist and jewelry designer, son of Charles Lewis Tiffany
- January 25 – Lewis J. Selznick, American film producer (b. 1870)
- January 29
    - Thomas Coward, English ornithologist (b. 1867)
    - Sara Teasdale, American lyrical poet (b. 1884)
- January 31 – John Galsworthy, English writer, Nobel Prize laureate (b. 1867)
- February 5 – Josiah Thomas, Australian politician (b. 1863)
- February 12
    - Henri Duparc, French composer (b. 1848)
    - Sir William Robertson, British Field Marshall (b. 1860)
- February 14 – Carl Correns, German botanist and geneticist (b. 1864)
- February 15 – Pat Sullivan, Australian-born director and producer of animated films (b. 1887)
- February 18 – James J. Corbett, American boxer (b. 1866)
- February 26 – Spottiswoode Aitken, Scottish-American actor (b. 1868)
- February 27 – Walter Hiers, American actor (b. 1893)

- March 1 – Uładzimir Žyłka, Belarusian poet (b. 1900)
- March 6 – Anton Cermak, Mayor of Chicago (assassinated) (b. 1873)
- March 10 – Ahmed Sharif as-Senussi, Chief of the Senussi order in Libya (b. 1873)
- March 14 – Balto, American sled dog (b. 1919)
- March 18 – Prince Luigi Amedeo, Duke of the Abruzzi, Italian mountaineer, explorer, and admiral (b. 1873)
- March 20 – Giuseppe Zangara, attempted assassin of Franklin D. Roosevelt (b. 1900)
- March 26 – Eddie Lang, American musician (b. 1902)

April–June

- April 4 – William A. Moffett, U.S. admiral (crash of airship USS *Akron* (ZRS-4)) (b. 1869)
- April 17 – Harriet Brooks, Canadian physicist (b. 1876)
- April 22 – Henry Royce, English car manufacturer (b. 1863)
- April 23 – Tim Keefe, American baseball player and MLB Hall of Famer (b. 1857)
- May 2 – Leonard Huxley, English writer (b. 1860)
- May 6 – Li Ching-Yuen, Chinese herbalist, martial artist, tactical advisor (b. 1677)
- May 13 – Ernest Torrence, Scottish actor (b. 1878)
- May 16 – John Henry Mackay, German writer (b. 1864)
- May 19 – Thomas J. O'Brien, American politician and diplomat (b. 1842)
- May 24
    - Ludovic Arrachart, French aviator (b. 1897)
    - Percy C. Mather, English Protestant missionary (b. 1882)
    - Rosslyn Wemyss, 1st Baron Wester Wemyss, British admiral (b. 1864)
- May 26 – Jimmie Rodgers, American country singer (b. 1897)
- June 2 – Frank Jarvis, American athlete (b. 1878)
- June 29 – Roscoe Arbuckle, American comedian (b. 1887)

July–September

- July 3 – Hipólito Yrigoyen, former President of Argentina (b. 1852)
- July 15
  - Irving Babbitt, American literary critic (b. 1865)
  - Freddie Keppard, American jazz musician (b. 1890)
  - Léon de Witte de Haelen, Belgian general (b. 1857)
- August 1 – Sulejman Delvina, Albanian politician, former Prime Minister (b. 1884)
- August 13 – Hasan Prishtina, Albanian politician, former Prime Minister (b. 1873)
- August 18 – James Williamson, Scottish film director (b. 1855)
- August 22 – Alexandros Kontoulis, Greek general (b. 1858)
- August 23
  - Marie Cahill, American singer and actress (b. 1870)
  - Adolf Loos, Austrian-Czechoslovak architect (b. 1870)
- September 2 – Francesco de Pinedo, Italian aviator (b. 1890)
- September 7 – Edward Grey, British statesman (b. 1862)
- September 8 – Faisal I of Iraq, king of Iraq
- September 10 – Giuseppe Campari, Italian opera singer and Grand Prix driver (b. 1892)
- September 20 – Annie Besant, English Theosophist, women's rights activist, writer and orator (b. 1847)
- September 25
  - Paul Ehrenfest, Austrian-Dutch physicist (b. 1880)
  - Ring Lardner, American writer (b. 1885)
- September 28 – G. R. S. Mead, British writer (b. 1863)

October–December

- October 5 – Renée Adorée, French actress (b. 1898)
- October 12 – John Lister, English politician (b. 1847)
- October 16 – Ismael Montes, 26th President of Bolivia (b. 1861)
- October 29
  - George Luks, American painter (b. 1867)

- o Albert Calmette, French bacteriologist and immunologist (b. 1863)
- November 3 – Émile Roux, French physician (b. 1853)
- November 5 – Texas Guinan, American actress (b. 1884)
- November 8 – Mohammed Nadir Shah, King of Afghanistan (b. 1883)
- November 16 – Kyrillos III of Cyprus, archbishop of the Cypriot Orthodox Church (b. 1859)
- November 30 – Arthur Currie, Canadian general (b. 1875)
- December 4 – Stefan George, German poet (b. 1868)
- December 8
  - o Karl Jatho, German airplane pioneer (b. 1873)
  - o John Joly, Irish physicist (b. 1857)
- December 16 – Robert W. Chambers, American writer (b. 1865)
- December 17 – Thubten Gyatso, 13th Dalai Lama (b. 1876)
- December 19
  - o George Jackson Churchward, Great Western Railway chief mechanical engineer (b. 1857)
  - o Friedrich von Ingenohl, German admiral (b. 1857)
- December 25 – Francesc Macià, President of the Generalitat (autonomous government of Catalonia) (b. 1859)
- December 26
  - o Eduard Vilde, Estonian writer (b. 1865)
  - o Anatoly Lunacharsky, Russian Marxist revolutionary (b. 1875)

Nobel Prizes

- Physics – Erwin Schrödinger, and Paul Adrien Maurice Dirac
- Chemistry – not awarded
- Physiology or Medicine – Thomas Hunt Morgan
- Literature – Ivan Alekseyevich Bunin
- Peace – Sir Norman Angell (Ralph Lane)

In the News.

Adolf Hitler declared his intentions for a state-sponsored "People's Car" program.

Machine gun is demonstrated by Japanese Scientist firing 1,000 shot per minute.

Strong winds strip the topsoil from the drought affected farms in Midwest creating Dust Bowls.

Albert Einstein emigrates to the United States from Germany.

Nearly every country in the world was suffering from high unemployment.

Adolf Hitler appointed Chancellor of Germany.

Adolf Hitler bans all other political parties turning Germany into a One Party State.

The film King Kong premieres during March.

Alcatraz becomes a federal penitentiary.

The Loch Ness Monster is sighted for the first time in modern times.

The Chocolate chip cookie is invented

The Board Game Monopoly is invented

1933 Calendar

January 1933
Sun	Mon	Tue	Wed	Thu	Fri	Sat
1	2	3	4	5	6	7
8	9	10	11	12	13	14
15	16	17	18	19	20	21
22	23	24	25	26	27	28
29	30	31				

February 1933
Sun	Mon	Tue	Wed	Thu	Fri	Sat
			1	2	3	4
5	6	7	8	9	10	11
12	13	14	15	16	17	18
19	20	21	22	23	24	25
26	27	28				

March 1933
Sun	Mon	Tue	Wed	Thu	Fri	Sat
			1	2	3	4
5	6	7	8	9	10	11
12	13	14	15	16	17	18
19	20	21	22	23	24	25
26	27	28	29	30	31	

April 1933
Sun	Mon	Tue	Wed	Thu	Fri	Sat
						1
2	3	4	5	6	7	8
9	10	11	12	13	14	15
16	17	18	19	20	21	22
23	24	25	26	27	28	29
30						

May 1933
Sun	Mon	Tue	Wed	Thu	Fri	Sat
	1	2	3	4	5	6
7	8	9	10	11	12	13
14	15	16	17	18	19	20
21	22	23	24	25	26	27
28	29	30	31			

June 1933
Sun	Mon	Tue	Wed	Thu	Fri	Sat
				1	2	3
4	5	6	7	8	9	10
11	12	13	14	15	16	17
18	19	20	21	22	23	24
25	26	27	28	29	30	

July 1933
Sun	Mon	Tue	Wed	Thu	Fri	Sat
						1
2	3	4	5	6	7	8
9	10	11	12	13	14	15
16	17	18	19	20	21	22
23	24	25	26	27	28	29
30	31					

August 1933
Sun	Mon	Tue	Wed	Thu	Fri	Sat
		1	2	3	4	5
6	7	8	9	10	11	12
13	14	15	16	17	18	19
20	21	22	23	24	25	26
27	28	29	30	31		

September 1933
Sun	Mon	Tue	Wed	Thu	Fri	Sat
					1	2
3	4	5	6	7	8	9
10	11	12	13	14	15	16
17	18	19	20	21	22	23
24	25	26	27	28	29	30

October 1933
Sun	Mon	Tue	Wed	Thu	Fri	Sat
1	2	3	4	5	6	7
8	9	10	11	12	13	14
15	16	17	18	19	20	21
22	23	24	25	26	27	28
29	30	31				

November 1933
Sun	Mon	Tue	Wed	Thu	Fri	Sat
			1	2	3	4
5	6	7	8	9	10	11
12	13	14	15	16	17	18
19	20	21	22	23	24	25
26	27	28	29	30		

December 1933
Sun	Mon	Tue	Wed	Thu	Fri	Sat
					1	2
3	4	5	6	7	8	9
10	11	12	13	14	15	16
17	18	19	20	21	22	23
24	25	26	27	28	29	30
31						

www.ingramcontent.com/pod-product-compliance
Lightning Source LLC
Chambersburg PA
CBHW061930280526
45787CB00004B/1550